Where is God when I can't find Him?

David Johnson

Copyright © 2013 David Johnson

All rights reserved.

ISBN:14922957704
ISBN-13:978-14922957706

DEDICATION

This book is dedicated to the memory of my parents, Willie and Martin Johnson, and for their instilling in me a deep and abiding respect for God's Holy Word.

CONTENTS

Part One: The Serpent

Part Two: The Great I AM

Part Three: What is Man?

Introduction to

"Where Is God When I Can't Find Him?"

It began as a conversation. But not just any conversation. It was a conversation between the supreme powers in the universe: Jehovah God and Satan.

In the book of Job God pulls back the curtain separating earth and heaven and lets us see the dramatic interworkings of forces in our world. The opening scene of the book reveals the conversation between God and Satan as they discuss Job. The rest of the drama in the book plays out against the backdrop of that conversation.

I don't believe that the book of Job describes a one-time incident involving one man. I believe it reveals to us the way the world works for all of us.

It is in the book of Job that we find the "Why?" questions that plague us. And the answers are revealed, too, though not in a way that is always satisfying to our desire to know details.

In the pages that follow I will discuss what we learn about the three main players in this drama, Satan, God, and man. My main focus will be on what we learn about each of them in the first two chapters. I suggest you read those two chapters slowly prior to reading the rest of this booklet. Jot down things that you notice. Write down questions that you have.

Let the message of Job increase your faith and confidence in walking with God while you journey on this earth.

- David Johnson

(PART ONE)
THE SERPENT

His Appearance

His odor arrives before he does. The noxious smell of sulfur causes the other angels to pinch their noses. They always hate it when he shows up. He reeks of putrification. And in spite of the eternal, brilliant light that shines from God's throne, there is a feeling of darkness emanating from him as he slowly inches his way forward.

When it is his turn to stand before God, his features are revealed in full detail – a pitted and scarred face; bushy eyebrows; lightless eye sockets; parched, cracked lips; a thick, dry tongue that constantly flicks in and out; broken and yellowed teeth; a body that continually morphs itself into indeterminate shapes and colors; cinders and ashes are scattered in his wake.

Suddenly the laser-like eyes of God turn onto the Great Deceiver and his thunderous voice shatters the uncomfortable silence that has fallen in heaven. "Satan, what have you been up to?"

Like a vampire caught by the sun's rays, Satan writhes. A grimace creases his features and a cry escapes from his throat. His dark eyes flit back and forth at the accusing gazes of the angelic throng surrounding the throne.

Beelzebub detests this part of his punishment for the rebellion he led eons ago. He's grown comfortable with his life in utter darkness, away from God's presence. But these periodic calls from God to give a public accounting of himself grate on him. It is humiliating to have to tell the Creator what he already knows, for experience has made it apparent that there are no secrets with him. He feels like a scarab pinched between thumb and forefinger.

It's like God wants to make a point with him of who is in control. To refuse to answer Jehovah's call is not an option.

Since before the great rebellion, Satan has known that his Achilles' heel is his prideful nature. He chokes and gags every time he appears in heaven because he knows he will be forced to swallow that bitter pill. He grits his teeth as he kneels before the King of the universe.

Application to Today

I'm glad Satan has to answer to God. I need to remember that. It's easy to look at all the destruction and chaos in this world (wars, mass killings, starvation) and believe that Satan is winning the war; that his influence is more powerful than any good that exists. Our faith can begin to waver in the face of such evidence.

And then, when the destruction and chaos touch us personally, we scream in agony, "Who's in control?!"

It's encouraging to me to know that periodically God grabs Satan and says, "Hey you. I'm in charge here. Not you. Let's talk about what you've been up to."

But I think that reminder is not so much for Satan as it is for me.

His Nature

Without looking up, Satan replies in a hollow, raspy voice, "I have been roaming throughout the earth, going back and forth on it." It is the verbatim answer he has given since the question was first posed following the creation of earth and the fall of man in the Garden of Eden.

Millenniums later, the apostle Peter will describe him as a beast that "prowls around like a roaring lion looking for someone he can devour." Contrary to popular myth, lions do not chase down the biggest and strongest in order to prove domination. They pick out the weakest of the heard and drag them down to be destroyed and eaten. They have a sixth sense about which ones will be the easiest targets.

Lions will shadow a herd of animals for hours and days, lying in wait, looking for an opening. They are indefatigable. Watching closely for a weakened animal's misstep, they, with lethal dispatch, drag it to its bloody demise.

Satan lives in the shadows of our lives, keeping close surveillance on our every move. His keen eyes will notice the slightest misstep or brief hesitancy in our gait.

Application to Today

My spirit weakens at times. It is part of my humanness. Whether it is struggling to pay bills, worrying about children and grandchildren, body aches and pains, or seeing those I care about in pain, my resolve is sometimes shaken.

Satan knows this about me. It sometimes seems that, next to God, Satan knows me better than anyone. That is why he is tireless, hoping I will give in to him. Nothing gives him more excitement that to see a weakened spirit or a head bowed in defeat. Once that faintness of spirit shows itself, he flattens his ears and creeps closer.

Having wounded me with the chaos he has created, he digs in for the kill shot. Lucifer licks his lips in anticipation of devouring another soul. He feasts on the wounded.

He remains consumed with one thing – the ruin of men's souls.

We should not underestimate our enemy.

What He Knows

Satan listens thoughtfully as God brags on his servant, Job, especially pointing out his integrity. Sucking on his teeth in an absentminded manner, the Serpent says, "Sure Job has integrity, but that's because you protect him and keep any harm from coming to him. But suppose, just suppose, you took away the things that matter the most to him – his family and his possessions. What do you think would happen? I say he'd curse you to your face."

Application to Today

Satan knows me by name.

He knows details about my life - who my family is; what my occupation is; where I live; what my banking account looks like; the condition of my physical health.

He knows what I value most in life. This knowledge allows him to know where I can be hurt the most. His view of this is these are my points of vulnerability. And he will not hesitate to attack me at those very points.

It is this knowledge of man that makes Satan so lethal and an opponent to be feared.

His Greed

Whereas lions in the wild only kill to satisfy their hunger, not for the pure joy of killing, this is where the comparison to Satan falls apart. For no matter how many screaming, tormented souls the Keeper of the Bottomless Pit has chained in the netherworld, he wants just one more.

And the more devoted a person is to God, the more enticing they are to the Devil. This is exactly why he sets his sights on Job.

The Evil One drops any pretense of saving face and turns to the very one who cast him out of heaven to grant his wish. So eager is he to get his talons in Job that he asks permission to have his way with him.

It is this exact kind of encounter that Jesus points out to Peter just before the betrayal. "Satan has asked to sift you as wheat."

Application to Today

Satan <u>wanted</u> Job!

He <u>wanted</u> Peter!

And he <u>wants</u> you and me! It is very possible that just today Satan came before the throne of God and asked for you by name.

No one is safe from his insatiable appetite for souls.

His Brazenness

The Devil, in an unbelievable display of brazenness, teases, tests and tempts Jehovah. He engages in a game of "I dare you."

Lucifer plays to the audience of assembled angels. Turning, he asks, "Does Job fear God for nothing? Have you not put a hedge around him and his household and everything he has? You have blessed the work of his hands, so that his flocks and herds are spread throughout the land. But now stretch out your hand and strike everything he has, and he will surely curse you to your face."

It amounts to his feeble attempt to "trick" God into playing a game of chicken with the life of Job. Satan calculates that Job is like many of the lost souls in Hades. They only followed God when things were going well. But when problems came, they turned their backs on God, not realizing that they were at that moment embracing Satan. "The only reason Job is devoted to God is because he appears to be living a charmed life," is Satan's line of reasoning.

Application to Today

Satan has no qualms and no shame about asking Jehovah for our soul.

No one is too important or too insignificant for him to set his sights on.

His plan of attack can range from simple, to complex, to audacious. And it will be specific to our situation, a battle plan drawn up in the dark recesses of the Devil's depraved mind.

His Limits

The Creator of the Universe considers Satan's proposal for a moment. He weighs the character of Job against the nature of The Adversary. He sees the possible outcomes before they exist. Then he says, "Very well, then, everything he has is in your power."

Satan throws back his head and howls in delight.

The angels cover their ears in pain at his shrieks.

The Tempter grins so broadly that his cracked lips show a trickle of blood.

Then, just before he makes his departure from God's presence to begin working on Job, he hears that dreaded word thundering from the throne of the king: "But – "

A scowl spreads across the Devil's face as he turns back to face The Ruler.

God points his finger at Satan and says, "But on the man himself do not lay a finger."

It is now Beelzebub's turn to gnash his teeth. This is another part of his curse that he hates. He is not all powerful. He cannot do any and everything he would like.

He vigorously shakes his head in an effort to escape the choking feeling tightening around his neck. Bowing low, through gritting teeth he responds, "As you say."

Application to Today

This one truth is perhaps the most comforting of all to me. In spite of the fact that Satan is a lion on the loose, he is also a lion with a collar around his neck and God is holding the other end of the leash. God puts limits on Satan.

Therefore, if I trust God to supply all the good in my life and to care for me, then I must trust him to know how much trouble to allow into my life. This is a difficult truth to accept and perhaps even harder to understand.

We think we know what is best for us. We know when we've had enough. So we cry out, "I can't take anymore!"

But God is in charge and he is a father who always knows best. He has weighed our character against the character of our Enemy and will always act in our best interest.

One word from him, exactly when it is needed, will stop Satan short.

His Power

Once Satan is given permission to attack Job, all the forces of hell are turned loose. "The oxen were plowing and the donkeys were grazing nearby, and the Sabeans attacked and made off with them. They put the servants to the sword."

Then fire rained down from the sky and destroyed all his sheep and the shepherds who were watching them. At the same time, "The Chaldeans formed three raiding parties and swept down on (Job's) camels and made off with them. They put the servants to the sword."

In his feverish dance of destruction, Satan then sent a hurricane force wind that killed Job's children.

Later, in round two of this battle over Job, The Tormentor "afflicted Job with painful sores from the soles of his feet to the crown of his head."

Application to Today

These scenes of destruction are difficult to explain except in the light of the immense power that Satan is allowed to wield. The holy record indicates that he has the power to influence people (the Sabeans and Chaldeans) to carry out his will; power over the forces of our weather; and power over diseases.

It staggers the imagination! Lots of "why's" and "how's" scream in our head at these assertions, none of which I can answer with certainty.

But if this story is true, and I believe it is and that it is not a parable of some kind, then we have no other conclusion besides these. We are forced to see the truth – next to God there is no more powerful force in the universe than Satan.

Therefore, oftentimes when disaster strikes, it is not God attacking us but rather Satan. Our anger toward our Father is

misguided. We should shake our fist at Our Adversary.

His Reach

When God first gives permission to Satan to "have his way with Job," only he can't touch Job himself, that does not slow the Devil down. It gives him no pause or hesitation. The answer is easy – strike the things that are most dear to Job's heart.

As I will point out later when I discuss Job, he was a family man. His children were his pearls, each one beautiful and precious in their own way. There was nothing he wouldn't do for them.

So, with the lethality of a heat-seeking missile, Our Adversary reaches out and touches this soft and tender side of Job. The light of life in these ten children is snuffed out when the house there are in collapses by the force of a mighty wind.

Of all the painful things that can happen to us during our walk on earth, there is no pain worse than the loss of a child. It boils out the marrow in our bones and sears our heart. Just to take a breath becomes an arduous task. Darkness swallows us up.

The righteous man Job is driven to his knees!

Application to Today

This is one of the scariest powers in Satan's arsenal. In his efforts to destroy me, he will pass right by me without even glancing in my direction and he will attack what is most dear to my heart – my family.

In many ways, at this point in my life, I don't so much fear what Satan can do to me. My life is nothing. To depart this earth would be a blessing beyond imagination. But I do fear what he can do to those I hold close in my heart.

I have witnessed the path of destruction left behind by this Grim Reaper. The shards of shattered hearts scattered on the floor of silent bedrooms. The emptiness of a life where hope is lost. Like the house of Mrs. Havisham in Dickens' <u>***Great Expectations***</u>*,* *time has stopped.*

Like Job's friends, I have sat with those in the grip of grief and found no words to offer that can ease the pressure weighing on their chest so that they can just get one breath. It is a helpless feeling.

His Depravity

Our Enemy is a sociopath. Look at this list of traits of a sociopath and see if you don't agree with me:

- Superficial charm
- Grandiose sense of self-worth
- Pathological lying
- Conning and manipulativeness
- Lack of remorse or guilt
- Callouseness and lack of empathy

Adolph Hitler, Saddam Houssein, John Wayn Gace, Ted Bundy, Son of Sam, the Green River Slayer are all names synonymous with evil. But none of them hold a candle to the author of their evil deeds – Satan!

Application to Today

We must never be guilty of thinking, "Oh Satan would never do that!" Our minds cannot comprehend the depths of darkness in his soul. He lives his life in pursuit of evil, in inventing new ways to express his total disregard for mankind.

Having lost his battle with God over the power of death when Jesus arose from the grave, the only pleasure The Serpent has left is the ruination of men's souls.

His Tenacity

As if all the previous traits we've looked at weren't bad enough, there is another trait that makes all of them worse – Satan does not give up easily. He is tenacious. If one tactic doesn't work, he doesn't simply give up and walk away. He tries another, then another, then another.

Even against Jesus Christ the Devil did not give up. He met Jesus in the desert at the very beginning of his ministry and tempted him to give up on his heavenly mission. But even though Christ defeated him, Luke 4:13 tells that when the Tempter had finished, he left him until a more opportune time. Satan never gave up looking for an opening, a weakness, in Jesus that would allow him to bring him to his knees.

Application to Today

I must always be on my guard. When I have come through the valley of the shadow of death and feel the sunshine on my face, I don't need to relax and think my testing is over.

Satan is not discouraged by my having won the battle. He is already reaching into his quiver, grasping an arrow, and fitting it on the taut string of his bow.

Even now he is taking aim.

(PART TWO)

The Great I AM

He Alone is Worthy of Worship

Light.

Brilliant, dazzling, blinding light.

Light so bright that "there is no need for the sun there."

Light so large that there are no shadows to be found. "And there is no night there."

This is a physical description of a spiritual being, but it is the closest thing to the truth that our finite minds can grasp.

The light is a manifestation of who he is and his nature. Perfect.

In the opening words of the book of job we learn that Job "feared God," reads the NIV. The Message explains it this way, "he was totally devoted to God."

The English word "fear" appears often in the Bible, especially in describing an attitude toward God. Our connotation of the word "fear" is usually a negative one. We think of it in terms of being afraid of the dark or being fearful of a monster – a child's view of the world.

It's this view that contributes to so many people viewing God in a negative light. He is the boogey man who's out to get you, eager to hurt you.

A more correct understanding of this word is that it indicates being in awe of someone or something, which is a far cry from being scared of it.

When I try to think of things on earth that I have been in awe of I'm reminded of: seeing the view from the top of Pike's Peak; witnessing the birth of our children; being a witness to people overcoming incredible odds to become a person of dignity, honor, and dedication.

"Awe" is a feeling of drop-jaw amazement. It leaves you speechless. This is how Job felt about God.

Just a few verses later (verse five), we see Job's feeling and attitude about God put into action. Any time his children engaged in a period of feasting, afterward Job would offer a sacrifice to God for each of them, just in case they had sinned toward God, even if only in their heart. He did this with regularity.

Job's attitude and actions are a demonstration of what we today would call worship. Job clearly believed that God was worth of being worshipped. It's probably fair to infer that God had even give Job instructions about how to approach Him.

In a discussion of worship I think it's very important to point out that God doesn't *need* to be worshiped, for God needs nothing.

We need worship. Worship's direction is toward God, but worship's benefit is for us. Worship is good for us.

However, when worship becomes more about those worshiping than the one worshipped, it has become adulterated.

I have carried the following quote in my songbook for decades. (I wish I could give credit to its author, but I have no recollection where I found it. So I beg forgiveness from the author.)

- "Worship is the occupation of the soul with God. By a deliberate act of will we focus our thoughts and feelings on God. We look with awe at His majesty. We are filled with wonder as we view His omnipotence. We stand amazed as we consider His perfect holiness. With reverence we think about His love. With gratitude we remember His mercy. This is what worship is: awe, wonder, amazement, reverence and gratitude."

Worship has certainly changed over the course of civilization. It's important to remember that all of the changes have been prompted by man's desires, not God's.

I'm not saying that all the changes have been right or wrong. I'm simply pointing out that what we view as "appropriate" ways of worshipping are often based on our own ideas about worship.

In the first century church music sounded nothing like it does today. There was no harmony. There was little variation in pitch, resulting in little attention to a melody. The closest thing we could use as a comparison would be Gregorian chants.

Depending on the listener, Gregorian chants are either boring or deeply meaningful, which means some people like them and some people don't.

I'm guessing that the first person who introduced simple two-part harmony in a worship setting was treated with extreme scorn. And that's the way it's been ever since.

Many battles have been waged between religions and within religions over what we should and should not do in worship. I'm probably going to disappoint you when I tell you that I am not going enter into that fray. That's not the point of this article.

My point is, do we have the same attitude in worship as Job did?

Are we eager and regular regarding the worship of God?

Do we have "awe, wonder, amazement, reverence and gratitude" when we approach God?

It is those elements of the heart that will make worship the meaningful experience God intended for it to be.

He Believes In You

The gauntlet was thrown down by Satan; thrown in the face of God.

"I know your creation better than you do," Satan taunts God. "You think Job is such a wonderful example of humanity, but let him experience trials and he'll turn his back on you. He only worships you because he's had no troubles. If you don't believe me, just give me a chance at him."

It is an audacious dare, a dare that comes from a heart of pride. It is a dare made by a psychopath.

Instead of dismissing Satan, God, ever the teacher, chooses, once again, to make a point with the Prince of Darkness. There seems to be no hesitation by God. As usual, He knows what he's doing.

"Very well, then," God says, "everything he has is in your power, but on the man himself do not lay a finger."

In that statement there hinges the balance of power between heaven and hell. Who best knows the heart of man – The Creator or The Deceiver?

Satan leaves the presence of God rubbing his hands together in eager anticipation, certain that he will finally win at least this one battle in the epic war he's waged against the one who threw him from the heavenly realms.

How could God, the Father of love and mercy, give permission to Satan to inflict so much pain on the man Job? He could do it because he *does* know this man's heart. He had complete confidence in Job to do the right thing, to make the right choices. God believed in Job.

God was giving Job an opportunity to demonstrate to Satan, and to himself, that all that matters is serving the Ruler of the Universe. The principle was not dependent on life circumstances.

A similar conversation takes place thousands of years after the one surrounding Job. Satan asks for permission to have his way with an impulsive, brash fisherman.

This time God is Immanuel and walking on the earth as a servant. So Jesus actually tells the fisherman, Peter, about the conversation, "Satan has asked to sift you like wheat," which, according to the metaphor, meant that Satan was going to flail him and throw him up into the wind.

So, just like Job, Peter was going to be given an opportunity to prove his loyalty in a crucible.

Sadly, Peter failed. Later that very night he denied ever knowing the Savior.

Thankfully his failure was not the final script. Jesus still has faith in Peter to make good choices. He even predicts the outcome. After telling Peter that Satan has asked for him, Jesus says, "But I have prayed for you, Simon, that your faith may not fail. *And when you have turned back*, strengthen your brothers." (emphasis mine.)

It's like Jesus says to Peter, "I know you're not going to be perfect. You're going to make some bad choices. But you're going to come through it. I still believe in you. I believe you will do the right thing."

It is a crucial point for me to remember when I am going through a crucible, when Satan has asked to sift me: God believes in me. I would never be placed there to begin with without Him having confidence in me to make good choices. It's like the coach placing the ball in your hands to take the final shot that will win the game.

What a confidence booster!

What an opportunity!

"You must spare his life."

In the epic battle between God and Satan for your soul, you should remember that it is a rigged fight. There is nothing fair about it. Satan is fighting with one arm tied behind his back.

When Satan received permission from God to tempt Job to turn away from God, he must have rubbed his hands in hellish glee and excitement. Ever since his fall from the angels in heaven Satan has looked for opportunities to get back at God, trying to prove him fallible, eager to show that God's plan is flawed.

Satan's vehicle for trying to accomplish this has always been mankind. Mankind stands as the pinnacle of God's miraculous power of creation, barely below the angels of heaven.

But as remarkable a creation as mankind is, mankind is flawed. The power of choice, being "free moral agents" it is called, is what sets us apart from all the rest of creation but also provides a toehold for Satan. In that place called "choice" we are able to reach toward God or turn our back from Him.

It's in that crevasse of "choice," that point of hesitation as we decide how we will perceive life, that Satan slips in and slings the sharp scythe called "Loss." Like he is walking through a field of ripened wheat, Satan's arm arches high over his head. The edge of the scythe glints in the sun. Suddenly Satan's arm sweeps toward the ground with the ferocity of a tornado. The follow through of the sharp blade sends it skyward in the other direction. In its wake, the brittle stalks of mankind topple to the ground severed from their roots by:

- Death of a child, a sibling, a parent, a spouse, a dear friend
- Divorce from the spouse they'd hoped to build a life with
- A devastating disease
- Business gone bankrupt
- Career that never took off

- Loss of a job and little opportunity of finding another
- Worldly possessions lost in a fire or a storm

For thousands of years Satan has believed that if our lives are filled with enough loss, we will become lost. That is the mission that continues to consume his every move.

Loss produces feelings of

- Despair
- Doubt
- Disbelief
- depression
- Anxiety
- Fear
- Hopelessness
- Uncertainty

So when he asked for permission to attack Job and God said yes, Satan was certain he would win. However, Satan must have gnashed his teeth when God put a qualifier on him.

God tells him, "Everything he has is in your power, *but* on the man himself do not lay a finger." (emphasis mine). God also tells him, "He (Job) is in your hands, *but* you must spare his life."

Why the restraints? Why put a leash on Satan? Because God does not want us destroyed. He knows us better than we do ourselves and "he will not let you be tempted beyond what you can bear." (I Corinthians 10:13).

Why God allows Satan to attack us is the subject for a separate article. For this one, I think it's important for us to remember that all of the chaos Satan creates in our world is nothing compared to how much he *could* cause if not for him being on a leash.

It's the choke collar on Satan that saves us.

Make Your Daddy Proud!

I was fortunate to be born to a father who loved me. Not that he was perfect, but he tried to do the right thing. And he loved me.

The one thing I never wanted to do was disappoint my dad. To hear the lecture that began, "I'm really disappointed in you" was to feel a pain worse that any spanking could leave.

I have friends who felt the same sentiment as me growing up – "Go ahead and beat me. Just don't give me 'the talk.'"

As bad as the feeling of disappointing my dad was, the feeling of making him proud was at the opposite swing of the emotional pendulum.

He was never shy when it came to boasting about his four children. His conversations with others would often begin, "Have I told you about David (or Martell or Steve or Paul)? Then he would launch into a, sometimes amplified, detailing of our latest efforts in life.

If pride could literally cause someone to pop a button off their vest, that would have been my dad.

To see his beaming face, to feel his strong hug, and to hear him say, "I'm so proud of you," would trigger a feeling of warmth in my heart that spread throughout my body. It was a feeling that would last for days or weeks.

Now that I've raised two daughters and have six grandchildren I understand even better why he felt so proud. Right or wrong, I feel like there is a piece of me in the lives of all them. It's like whatever they do is a reflection of me.

Through them I can achieve things that I could never do on my own.

All this is what makes God's statement to Satan in Job 1:8 so fascinating to me. Listen to what he says: *Then the LORD said to*

Satan, "Have you considered my servant Job? There is no one on earth like him; he is blameless and upright, a man who fears God and shuns evil."

Honestly, that sounds like something my daddy would have said to someone about his children. (And we would have been embarrassed at his use of hyperbole.)

Do you hear the pride in God's voice? Can you sense the satisfaction he felt about how Job was turning out?

This must have been a longstanding point of contention between God and Satan. Satan coming to report to God about all the sin and evil in the world, taunting God with things like, "There's not a redeemable quality in these humans you created," "They are worthless and useless," "They are just like me, full of evil," "Why waste time being involved with them?"

God would say, "No you're wrong Satan. There is good in them. And there are people who have chosen to live godly lives, unlike you. For instance, look at......"

Each time God would have an example to hold in Satan's face, Satan would grind his teeth in anguish, thinking, *"Why does He always find the good in people?!"*

I wonder if God ever told Job that he was proud of him? Did he ever tell Job about his conversation with Satan?

I like to think that he did. He certainly did when Jesus was on the earth, "This is my son whom I love..."

What would it feel like to have God whisper in your ear, "I'm proud of you"?

In the end, isn't that all that will matter? Is God proud of me, or not?

I suppose that's all I should be concerned about as I journey through my brief stay on earth, "Am I making my Daddy proud?"

If I'll focus on that, everything else will fall into place.

"God, where are you?!"

The psalmist David penned the words, "My God, my God why hast thou forsaken me?" (Ps 22:1). But they were immortalized when Christ yelled them from the cross in the last hours of his life.

It is a universal question. It has come from the lips of both devout believers and avowed atheists.

It has existed since the beginning of time. Even Job, in the midst of his suffering, wondered.

Interestingly, the question never comes from our lips when things are going well.

When did it happen for you?

- When you lost your job?
- When your spouse left you for another?
- When your child wandered into "the far country" and never returned?
- When your body was attacked by disease that was unrelenting?
- When your child died?
- When someone you loved lay suffering for weeks and months on end?
- When, as a child, you were abused by those who were supposed to protect you?

It is only in the darkest hours of our lives that the question finds its way into our heart and bubbles to the surface. In those scary times our feeling of aloneness is so severe that it pushes faith to the side and pulls up doubt to replace it.

Doubt. It is one of Satan's best weapons. It's the one he used in the Garden with Adam and Eve. "I know what God said, but...." And the seed of doubt was planted.

If Satan can cause us to doubt God's word or His presence in our lives, our heart will grow cold and angry or indifferent toward God.

Because we have the advantage of reading Job's biography, we are aware that God was present every step of the way with Job. Job couldn't see him, but we can see God was there. And while we might not understand why God acted the way He did, it is clear that He was in control of the entire drama.

The same thing happened when God's children were living as slaves for the Egyptians. As we read their story we find these words, "The Israelites groaned in their slavery. God heard their groaning. God looked on the Israelites and was concerned about them."

And yet forty more years passed before God sent Moses to lead them out of slavery. God told Moses, "I have indeed seen the misery of my people. I am concerned about their suffering. I have come down to rescue them."

In all, God's children were in Egypt for 430 years. 430 years!! How many generations died with the question on their lips, "God, where are you?!" Many died not realizing that He was where He always had been – everywhere.

Maybe your response to all this is, "If God is there, then why doesn't/didn't He do something?!"

We have finally arrived at the crux of the matter. This is what it is all about. We want to control what happens in our life. We want to be the Director on the set and bark out the orders to the players. Because if we were in charge of things, we can see very clearly what we would do to make things right. If we were in charge, life would be painless or at least less painful.

Volumes have been written on the value of pain, what can be learned or gained from painful experiences, or why God allows bad things to happen to good people. All of these books are man's efforts to make sense of this world.

But I wonder if we are really supposed to make sense of this world.

To be able to explain the how and why of everything would require us to have the mind of God.

To survive the vicissitudes of life with our faith intact sometimes requires us to ease back and rest in the place we call trust, even though it may feel illogical to do so.

We must remember that in the darkest of midnights, God is still present.

And he is still in control.

RIDE THE MORNING WINDS

By Grace Hawthorne

A frightening place, this world of ours,

The frantic pace of changing powers

Where no one plays familiar roles.

But in these days one promise holds.

I can ride the morning wind and You are there.

I can sail the widest seas and you are there.

I can find the darkest night and you are there.

I can never be lost from you.

(PART THREE)

What is Man?

We Can Live an Upright Life AND Be Wealthy and Powerful

The list is endless: John F. Kennedy, Richard M. Nixon, Bill Clinton, Jimmy Swaggart, Jim and Tammy Baker, Bernie Madoff, Jerry Sandusky, Joe Paterno. Powerful people with fatal character flaws.

Is it the seduction of power that has lead to their downfall? Did they sacrifice their principles in order to reach their positions?

Our eyes are teased into leering at the headlines on papers and magazines at checkout lines that purport the latest scandal involving someone sleeping with someone else's spouse.

An honest confession: I haven't watched t.v. news in probably a year. I got tired of it sounding like the latest episode of Rush Limbaugh or Jerry Springer. Do I really need all the dirty little details of people's lives? Maybe it's because in my line of work I hear those sorts of things regularly that I don't feel the urge to perk up my ears at the latest popular figure whose clay feet have been exposed.

Oh, I do keep up with what's going on in the world. I'm not a hermit. But I limit it to online news – CNN and USAToday. I look at the title of articles and then decide what if I want to read further. (My one concession to "paper" newspaper is my town's weekly newspaper, The McKenzie Banner. It's full of good news about people in our community.)

I'm afraid that a malaise has spread so thickly on us that we've come to believe (and accept) that no one can live a good life. It has permeated our moral fiber. So why even try?

The other horn of the devil's twist on truth is that *good* people can't get ahead. "If you want to be successful (i.e. wealthy and powerful), you have to cheat."

It is often the case that the older I get I find what I believe runs contrary to popular opinion. I believe we *can* live an upright life *and* be wealthy and powerful.

The oldest book in the Bible, the book of Job, describes its main character in these words. "This man was blameless and upright; he feared God and shunned evil."

Let me quickly clarify that "blameless and upright" doesn't mean he was perfect. Only one person who lived on earth was perfect and there hasn't been another since. (I apologize to all you narcissistic readers for bursting your bubble.)

Job was a man who made good choices. Serving God and pleasing him were his main goals in life. He tried hard to resist temptation. He battled Satan toe-to-toe and did not cave into his demonic efforts to get him to turn his back on God.

Job had moral fiber.

But not only did he have moral fiber, he was wealthy and powerful. Listen to this description: "He owned seven thousand sheep, three thousand camels, five hundred yoke of oxen and five hundred donkeys, and had a large number of servants. He was the greatest man among all the people of the East."

The phrase "had a large number of servants" may qualify as one of the biggest understatements in the Bible! Can you imagine how many servants it took to manage his herds, then the number of servants it took to feed those servants, then the number of servants it took to raise the crops to feed everyone, then the number of armed servants it took to protect the people, livestock and property from marauding armies?!

In a time when wealth was determined by who and what you owned, Job was rich beyond measure.

It is not money that corrupts, nor is it power that corrupts. It is the love of either that makes the drink poison.

I don't think it is coincidental that the description of Job as one who fears God was mentioned before the evidence of his wealth and power was listed.

If serving God comes first in our life, then whatever comes after that will not shake us or destroy us.

You Can Be Successful in the World and Successful with Your Family, Too

It seems like it's axiomatic that if you are successful in your career that it will come at the expense of your family life. We are frequently told of highly successful individuals who walk away from their career in order to devote more time to their families. The unspoken message is that it is impossible to do both at the same time.

I have certainly heard many people speak with great regret about actually losing their families because they neglected them while pursuing their dream of a career. And adults have related to me their bitterness toward a parent that neglected them as a child because of the demands of their job.

But it really doesn't have to be that way; doesn't have to be an either/or proposition.

Job is described as both a successful business man (extremely wealthy) and as someone extremely devoted to his family (he regularly offered sacrifices to God on their behalf).

What it takes to make it work is balance achieved through proper priorities.

> Gordon MacDonald wrote a book forty years ago titled <u>Ordering Your Private World</u>. It is about achieving balance in living. MacDonald suggests our life is divided into five parts:
>
> - Motivation
> - Use of Time
> - Wisdom and Knowledge
> - Spiritual Strength
> - Restoration.
>
> He reasons that if we spend too much time working on one area or if we neglect any area, our lives will be out of balance and

cause us problems.

It is a skewed life that causes successful people to lose their families, not their success.

Dr. Paul Faulkner wrote a book titled <u>Achieving Success Without Failing Your Family</u>. The book is the result of interviews he did with thirty couples and their children. These thirty couples had achieved great success in the business world while also maintaining a close-knit family.

Dr. Faulkner identified the following principles that guided these parents:

- Parenting on purpose
- Instilling values
- Loving and adoring their children
- Being a servant (leading from the foot of the table)
- Giving the gift of laughter
- Being transparent (communicating openly and honestly)
- Holding them tight and then turning them loose
- Coping positively with tragedy and failure

No matter what stage you are in raising your family, these two books will be very helpful to you.

Good Grief – It's Personal

She was a simple, unadorned young woman. Her long, awkward strides took her quickly from the door of my office to the couch. She plopped unceremoniously onto the couch and crossed her legs, swinging it impatiently as I settled into my chair.

Before I could open my mouth, she said, "My doctor says I need to be here. I think *he* needs to be here."

With that double-handful of words she's thrown at me she's told me much:

- She has some kind of emotional or behavioral symptoms that are significant enough that a primary care physician has noticed them and felt they needed addressed
- This woman takes the shortest route to a destination. She will not tolerate beating around the bush. I will have to be direct with her.
- She's mad at her doctor for insisting that she come.
- But has a tremendous amount of respect for her doctor to agree to do something she doesn't want to do.
- She has lots of misgivings about the value of counseling in general and is probably suspicious of me.

I decide to try a question. "So why would your doctor think you need to come see me?"

She grabs that question like a rodeo cowboy wrestling a calf to the ground. She holds the back of her hand toward me with one finger sticking up. No, it wasn't that finger. It was her ring finger. Pointing to the wedding ring encircling it, she says, "Doc tells me I need to take this off and get on with my life."

Folding her arms across her chest, her leg shifts into high gear again, swinging vigorously. There is an air of finality about her, as if she's said all she intends to say and now it's my turn.

Clearly I'm going to need some more information. So I venture another question, "So why don't you tell me your story?"

She gives a huff of exasperation. But she uncrosses her legs, leans forward and does indeed tell me her story.

Three years ago her husband was killed in a work related accident. He was thirty-four. So, at the age of twenty-eight she was a widow with four year old twin daughters and an eight month old son.

She concludes her story by saying, "Am I still sad sometimes? Yes. But I'm not depressed. I go to work every day. I take care of my kids and my house. But doc says I need to take this ring off."

Grief. It's an interesting word. It's an effort to describe in one word a myriad of emotions. Grief is not pain. It is our emotional response to pain; the specific kind of pain associated with loss.

The Hebrew word that is often translated "grief" in our Bibles simply means "suffering." Grief certainly represents the pinnacle of human suffering.

When any conversation revolves around human suffering, the name of Job inevitably shows up. It is hard to find any example of someone who experienced more loss that this ancient man. As a matter of fact, so shocking were the losses that Job experienced that when his friends came to see him, "they sat down with him upon the ground seven days and seven nights, and none spake a word unto him: for they saw that his grief was very great." Job 2:13

All emotions are internal but they need an external (physical, behavioral) expression, a means of finding their way out of the heart. For example, if you are happy, the corners of your mouth turn up producing a smile; you might laugh and even produce tears.

Finding a healthy way of expressing intense feelings is crucial to our mental health. As a matter of fact it is the holding in of emotions that causes a plethora of problems and constitutes one of the main reason counselor's offices are so busy.

Among the many things that impress me about Job is he readily and openly expressed his grief. What was Job's physical, behavioral response to his pain? He "tore his robe and shaved his head." He sat in a pile of ashes and "took a piece of broken pottery and scraped himself with it."

It is a vivid picture of someone giving full vent to their emotions. Am I saying we should all express our grief the same way Job did? No.

As a matter of fact I rarely offer any suggestions on how to express grief because I believe grief is the most personal experience a person can have. I try to stay out of the way of other's personal expression of grief. Everyone has to do things in ways that make sense to them, not to me.

The only time I am concerned about how a person is grieving is if, after a month or so, it is preventing them from functioning on a daily basis. That doesn't mean I think they should be over their loss in a month or so. (See my previous article "When Am I Going to Get Over This?"). I'm simply saying that it might be time to consider medications and/or behavioral changes.

Two points I'm trying to make here:

- Don't let someone tell you how you should be processing your grief or what "stage" you should be in.
- Don't make the mistake of telling someone what they should do with their grief just because it makes sense to you. Many people have been greatly wounded by well intentioned suggestions from others.

And the lady I mentioned in the opening of this article? What did I tell her? I simply asked her if she wanted to take her wedding ring off. Coupled with a colorful adjective, she said, "No."

"Then don't take it off," I replied. "That's your business what you do with your ring."

She responded with a warm, genuine smile. "Thank you. That's what I needed to hear." She added with laugh, "Just wait until I see that crazy doctor of mine."

Why Not Me?

He had lost everything – everything! His business, his employees, all his assets, property, even his children. Yes, children, as in plural. All dead.

Then he lost his health. Disease racked his body.

Job. His name is synonymous with suffering. Has there ever been anyone who has lost as much?

I return again and again to look at him. How did he do it? How did he survive with his faith intact?

What can I learn from him that I can share with others who suffer?

What is the path that he followed that I can imitate so that I can survive with my faith intact during the storms of life?

There is a tête-à-tête between Job and his wife early in the story. She seems to be fed up with his stoic stance in the face of such suffering. Perhaps she can't stand to see her husband in such physical pain. In a moment of raw emotion she screams at him, "Why don't you just curse God and die?!"

I ask myself the same question. Why didn't Job curse God, yell at him in fury, shake his fist in anger, or walk away from God?

That's what we do, isn't it?

Every time I come to this point in Job's drama I sit on the edge of my seat and cock my head a little to the side so I don't miss what he says. Tell me Job, what is the answer?

Listen with me to the child-like faith of this man as he gives the solution for us all to follow. It is a summation of his view of life. "Shall we accept good from God, and not trouble?"

Job, that man of ancient time, understood the nature of grace before it was revealed in its fullness by the gift of Christ to the world. He knew that every good thing that had ever happened in his life was because of the hand of God; God's grace-filled hand. Job understood that he didn't deserve any of the good in his life. He was an imperfect and flawed man. Yet his life was filled to overflowing with richness and blessings from God. Job had not earned these things. It was a gracious God that blessed him with them. Job asked the "Why me?" question when he was being blessed.

Many in that part of the world no doubt envied Job and his riches and position of power prior to calamity befalling him. Apparently his wife, too, enjoyed the sumptuous life they lived.

Actually it's what we all want. We want to be standing under the cup of blessing when it is being poured out. We eagerly soak it up and smile at our good fortune.

But when the cup dries up we want to pick up our divining rod and look for more promising ground.

While we today are prone to cry out, "Why me?", Job provides the counterpoint by saying, "Why not me?"

Job says to me that all our days come from God's hand, both the good days and the bad days. We can't be like children who are only content when they get what they want. We can't be God's fair weather friend.

If we are ready to receive a good day, we must be ready to receive a bad day. They come from the same hand.

The wise man, Solomon, put it in a very similar way when he wrote, "When times are good, be happy; but when times are bad, consider this: God has made the one as well as the other."

It explains how Job could say, "The Lord gives and the Lord takes away. Blessed be the name of the Lord." Job didn't love God because God was good to him. If he had, then he would have cursed God when things went badly.

Job loved God simply because he was God. That was how he

survived Satan's attack with his faith intact. That is the path that I must follow, too.

Conclusion

In the closing scenes of this dramatic play (beginning in chapter thirty-eight), Job and God are alone, face to face. Job is struggling to understand the universal question found on the lips of everyone who has faced trying times: "Why?"

The Father knows the question in the heart of his child and chooses to paint a picture as a means of explaining the answer to Job's question. The brush strokes he uses are questions – scores of questions. On and on God goes asking questions as Job stands mute and dumbfounded because the hues of the paints are beyond description and explanation.

- Where were you when I laid the earth's foundations?
- Have you ever given orders to the morning?
- Have you journeyed to the springs of the sea or walked in the recesses of the deep?
- Where is the way to the abode of light and where does darkness reside?
- Have you entered the storehouses of the snow?
- Do you know the laws of the heavens?
- Who endowed the heart with wisdom or gave understanding to the mind?
- Do you give the horse his strength?
- Does the hawk take flight by your wisdom?

Then in chapter forty God pauses in his interrogation of Job, pauses to chastise him. "Will the one who contends with the Almighty correct him? Let him who accuses God answer him!"

But by this point, the weight of God's unanswerable questions has driven Job to his knees. He answers, "I am unworthy – how can I reply to you? I put my hand over my mouth. I spoke once but I have no answer – twice, but I will say no more."

Having made his point to Job, God cuts to the quick and lays bare the genesis of Job's "why" questions. He tells Job that if he could answer God's questions, "Then I myself will admit to you that your own right hand can save you." Job, like all of us, wants to be in control, to organize the world's events according to his idea of right and wrong. We, too, want to call the shots, to do things in ways that make sense to us.

As much sense and order there is in the world, there is much in the world that makes no sense. And that is what we are left with – the part that makes no sense. We sit with it in our lap. We turn it over and over, studying every cut facet to find discernment, and are still left with questions.

So Job stands, as it were, naked before God, with no more questions. All he has left is his faith that God truly knows best and will do what is right. And he says to God, "I know that you can do all things; no plan of yours can be thwarted. You asked, 'Who is this that obscures my counsel without knowledge?' Surely I spoke of things I did not understand, things too wonderful for me to know."

About the Author

David Johnson spent fifteen years as a Youth and Family Minister. He then went back to school and received a Master's Degree in Social Work from the University of Tennessee. For the past twenty years he has been a Marriage and Family Therapist.

He has had positions as the Clinical Director at the Christian Counseling Center of Western Kentucky; the Treatment Director at Spirit Lake Recovery; and is presently a counselor at the McKenzie Medical Center.

David is Licensed as a Marriage and Family Therapist and as a Master Social Worker.

He has conducted numerous marriage retreats and workshops. He's been interviewed on both radio and television.

David has been married for forty years and has two daughters and six grandchildren.

In his spare time he is the Director of the David Johnson Chorus.

Connect with David by visiting his website: www.davidjohnsonbooks.com and learn about all his other books that have been published.